Emma Lou Thayne

"The hallmark of her life—as a woman, as a writer—is balance. She seems to have a stability and steadiness that could be traced to the equilibrium of her early home life . . . she may have become the voice of her people and culture."

Deseret News

"Emma Lou Thayne seems exultant…her sensitivity to the texture of language, her absolute harmony with nature, her unwavering faith in the human spirit…"

Marriage and Family
St. Abby Press

"…leaps all sorts of hurdles without even noticing them…to square fundamental values with reality…"

Salt Lake Tribune

"Emma Lou Thayne's poems are honest and strong, written in images bright with mountain freshness…pulls us deep into our own rememberings. We come away knowing we have read poems that are mature and important."

Ann Stanford

Books by Emma Lou Thayne

Spaces in the Sage
Until Another Day for Butterflies
The Family Bond
On Slim Unaccountable Bones
Never Past the Gate, a Novel
A Woman's Place
How Much for the Earth?
As for Me and My House
Things Happen
    Poems of Survival
All God's Critters Got a Place in the Choir
    (with Laurel Thatcher Ulrich)
Hope and Recovery
    A Mother-Daughter Story of Manic Depression and
    Bulimia (with Becky Thayne Markosian)
The Place of Knowing, A Spiritual Autobiography
    (Audio)

with love *Mother*

EMMA LOU THAYNE

DIGITAL LEGEND

New York 2010

Digital Legend Press, 2010
Deseret Book Company, 1975

© 2010 Emma Lou Thayne
All rights reserved. No part of this publication may be reproduced, stored in a retrieval system, or transmitted, in any form or by any means, electronic, mechanical, photocopying, recording, or otherwise, without the prior written permission of the publisher.

Digital Legend Press
New York Office
4700 Clover St.
Honeoye Falls, NY 14472

ISBN: 978-1-934537-82-4

www.digitalegend.com

1-877-222-1960

Printed in the United States of America

Cover Design by: Kim Blackett
Photo by: Tom Smart

Contents

With Love, Mother	1
First Loss	13
Gentle Then	15
I Marry You	13
To My Newborn Child	17
Child's Play	19
Sisters Giggling Somewhere	20
Quick Freeze	21
The Good hurt	21
To Daughters Eight and Ten	22
The Generation Gap	22
Letter to a Daughter	23
Goodnight	30
Cure	31
Hold	32
Mother's Day	33
Lesson #1	34
Somewhere My Children	36
Son-in-Law	37
Prospect: My Child with Child	38
Here I Love You	39
Bathing a First Grandchild, Three Months Old, at the Cabin	40
Gift	42

With Love, Mother

My mother and I were alone in her room in our house and she was dying. We both knew she was, but neither gave any indication of knowing. It would have clouded the assurance that each of us had always given the other–that things work out. That assurance of the goodness of life, of people, and of Heavenly Father was at the heart of our need now to comfort each other in the parting that loomed there like a thunderstorm, the kind of storm that Mother had prayed away when any of us were traveling and she was "working on the weather."

But now there was no staying the inevitable. That last day, on the 23rd of December, had started like the others with a bath, a sponge bath, of course, but a touching ritual that had lent us a closeness long lost in the routine of adulthood. Just before Thanksgiving Mother had suffered a massive heart attack. After three weeks of intense hospital care, it had become apparent that the damaged heart would never be able to pump the fluid from her lungs and she would die, maybe in a day, maybe in a…No one really knew. So we brought her home to the rooms she loved in the home she had built with us fifteen years before when my father died at fifty-nine.

Our house had become hers, our lives and those of our five daughters a running, hectic, noisy, and very alive part of her dailiness. Until the day she went to the hospital she had been a vital participant in our lives and in those of scores of others, family and friends, who now came to her with a terrible need to hold.

It was the need that eased my hand under the washcloth across her shoulders and down her arms. Bathing her was somehow a return to the essentials of human contact. She was tiny – only 4 feet 10 inches, barely to the neckties of my father, husky brothers, and husband – and her body was like a baby's – soft, plump, white, smooth, and without a blemish. I laughed as I washed her feet and rubbed fresh-smelling powder on her back, telling her, "You're marvelous, Mother. You take me back to bathing my babies, to all the delight in making them sweet and clean."

And I'd pat her and smooth her nightie and make sure her pillow was fluffed just right against her cheek. She'd smile too – even that day – and take my hand covered in powder and lotion and grip it thumb to thumb, letting me feel her affirmation flood into my palm and up my arm and into my soul. If ever there were a bond between mother and daughter, it was there in that bath time, growing firm and tight for anything that might come.

In the days since, I've thought often of how that all worked as I've looked at my own girls and pondered the reasons for good and no-so-good times together. It seems that a lot of having what psychologists call "a great mother-daughter relationship" is dependent upon my being able—and I do assume almost all of the responsibility for what happens between us—to maintain the kind of warm obvious, gentle concern for them that I exhibited when they were babies and I had the joyful job of giving them a bath.

This may appear ridiculous. How can a mother sustain that feeling of active guardianship throughout the life of her growing, independent, challenging daughters? How can she continue to demonstrate in concrete ways that she still cherishes them? The actual process of washing and anointing with love goes with childhood, as does the need for the kind authentic motherliness. But between any one of my daughters and me there is a tremendous need to explore and keep alive on a very daily basis those elements that made that early association so satisfying for both of us.

I do think it's possible. It involves all of the miracle of being human and demands a constant sharing between me as a mother and each of my daughters, in all five areas of human potential– the physical, the emotional, the mental, the social, and the spiritual.

First, the physical. How easy it is to forget in our relationships with a child the power of touch. I remember when each of my girls was tiny how I couldn't hug her tight enough or rock her long enough or soothe her softly enough. What makes me think that same touch has lost its magic for either of us? True, a lot of that kind of touching is lost in the mere process of growing up, but I can still pat her shoulder when she looks as if she needs it or squeeze her when she's glad or sad, and keep in touch all the time. And what better than a good-night kiss to seal the day with I love you?

Then there's the emotional. When each of my daughters was small I was in on her every hurt or excitement. When she came running to me while I was gardening, saying, "Mommy, butterflies scare me," I held her and smiled the fear away. What difference should it make if now she's afraid of going to a new school or of breaking up a current romance or of the awesomeness of thinking about marriage? And if the sharing of traumas draws me closer to her, why shouldn't I tell her about mine and allow her the privilege of smiling me out of them—or at least of hearing them and understanding me better?

Someone once said that the greatest disservice we do each other is to give the constant appearance of "normalcy." No one is free of weakness, failure, ineptitude, anxiety. To participate in the emotional life of my child, I must be willing to accept her problems without condemnation and to share mine with her without needing the status of the all-knowing, all-powerful, always-in-control grown-up. It is her humanness and ability to feel, to laugh, to cry, that draw me to her. Why not let that communion work actively for both of us?

And why not preserve perhaps our greatest outlet for tension—laughter? Always we've laughed. I remember getting the giggles during a violin recital when she was ten, and chuckling at the antics of the puppy or at the embarrassment of my falling flat on the ice in a group of strangers. What pleasant, binding exchange can we now have simply in laughing together? In trading stories of the day or breaking up over the crazy happenings in a wild household just before leaving on a trip?

In the sharing of frailty and laughter, my mother was always there to listen and to tell and to laugh, almost more and more as the years drew us both into womanhood and its complexities. And more and more her understanding brought me to her for the intimacy of sharing grief and joy.

Now what about the mental? When my daughter was a child I loved to teach her, to learn with her–how to draw a monkey, how to put the visible man together, what words were, why the sum came up. And now that she's a "people," there are horizons neither of us has explored. What finer meat for my mental mill than her saying, "Read this, Mother, You'll like it. And I want to talk to you about it."

Am I disqualified, because we are now one adult to another, from reading what she's written–a paper or report–and gleaning as well as constructively criticizing? By sharing the intellectual–books, concerts, plays, art, ideas (maybe not always together, but the same ones when possible)–we cultivate awareness not only of our world but of each other and our responses to that world. In consensus or divergence we can foster vast areas of interest that will pull us together for talk and stimulation. Mother never lost interest in life or in me and was always my severest and most sought-after critic–of what I read, what I thought, what I saw, what I believed. I needed her.

About the social. When she was young, my little girls and I went everywhere together. She absorbed my feelings for people in the grocery store, at meetings, in the houses around the block. Then when she went on her own, a birthday party, a Primary class, a bike ride were subject to detailed and exuberant accounting. We shared it all. And in depth. How more likely then to indicate my continued cherishing of her than to care–really care–about all that: About who said what to whom at school, about why she's jumping when the phone rings tonight, about the possible disaster of going or not going to that out-of-town formal.

And what insight might she have into adult workings if I mention the crisis in that class I taught today, or the funny situation at the meeting last night, or the poignant struggle of that friend in trouble this afternoon? How urgent can our need to confide be if we give each other current specifics from our lives and refuse to float apart on inch-deep generalities?

In another social way, we have the beautiful right to lend to each other's lives the people who occupy ours. In my mother's death I realized more than ever how she had exercised the right. Her friends are mine because she made me feel an important part of her life with them. In the same way she made my friends hers. One of my oldest friends said not long ago, "One reason I always liked to come to your house was that I never felt that I was just your friend. I felt like your parents and your brothers all thought of me as their friend too–and that made me more welcome than anything." What more expansive gift is there than my daughter's giving me her friends–boys and girls–to broaden my base? And what better can I give her than genuine companions from my sphere who will care about and coddle her into and through adulthood as my mother's friends did me? What range, what diversity, what depth we can hand to each other through the people that we love!

Finally, there is the spiritual. When my little girl wandered about crocuses in the spring or the taste of snow or the speed of a hummingbird outside the cabin, I relished the chance to marvel with her at the glory and the Giver. Throughout the day, by the bed and at the table, we shared every prayer of gratitude and supplication. My feelings about divinity and grace were hers through telling and example. I made sure she knew of my profound need for strength beyond myself, and of my easy faith that it was there. Almost by osmosis she sensed and enjoyed the rites and privileges of believing.

What makes me suppose that such osmosis is not still a strengthening product of expressing to each other what we feel about our spiritual soundings? Can she tell me how she felt about that talk or someone's seeming hypocrisy or someone else's fine sensitivity? Can we talk about what Jesus might have done in a touchy situation that confronts me? Can she share a Sunday School lesson at the table or expect my during-the-day prayers to be for her when a big test is in the offing? Do we have access to each other's spiritual make-up so that it is as real and operative in bringing us together as fixing a meal in the same kitchen might be?

On that last day, my mother's hand in mind, I found a new feeling for a continuity and faith. Through her lifetime of "working on the weather," of praying us through crises, of showing us how to give–goods, time, interest ourselves–of demonstrating a caring, laughing, loving, expectant way to go, Mother had done it all. She had preserved believing and had led us quietly and happily in the paths of righteousness by making those paths flower with fun and good spirit and camaraderie. Whatever storms there had been had been met with the certainty that they would pass, and that like Job, where we could not control our circumstances, we could control our responses.

And now I was loving her, my Grace, my pillar, my soft lady with the lamp. I leaned close to her, concerned that she hear, as she always had, my concern. I'd been a daughter different by far from the one I'd always imagined her wanting–a needlepoint, demure daughter more like her than my athletic, involved father. We'd joked about it before, but now I said, "Mother I know you've always wished I'd take a gentler horse."

She opened her brown eyes, flashing in dark circled settings, squeezed my hand harder, and said, "No. I've always loved you on the wild one."

And there it was. The whole secret of why she succeeded as a mother and why the bond of that moment held us firm. In every way she treasured me–physically, emotionally, mentally, socially, spiritually. She loved me as a person, as a unique, functioning, floundering potential, as truly a child of God. In spite of my failings, my impetuousness, my differences from her, our differences over the years, she loved me. And she showed it, always. She loved me as an adult just as she did when I was a little girl. She knew how to let her love mature and take on the dimension of whatever stage we both were in. Then along the way she let me go, gave me the honor of being myself, knowing that that was the surest way to bring me always back.

That night just before Christmas I had to let her go. While smiling at some flowers that had just arrived, Mother gasped and was gone. Alert and wise to the end, she remained my link with how to do it. And now, are more even than when he was here, she courses through me as a presence in everything I do. And now, far more even than when she was here, she courses through me as a presence in everything I do. And I'll keep going back and back to her and her memory for constant help in trying to see that my five girls grow up as I did–with love, Mother.

First Loss

My grandma shared her bed with me
Till she died when I was twelve.
We slept with breaths that matched.
I went to sleep every night restraining
Deliberately one extra breath in five
To let her slower time teach mine to wait.

She never knew I waited, but talked
To me of Mendon where Indians ferreted
Her isolated young-wife home for cheese and honey,
And of Santa Barbara and eerie tides that
Drew her now for gentle months away from snow,
And sometimes of Evangeline lost in the forest primeval.

Grandma's batter-beating, white-gloved, laughing
Daytime self slept somewhere else, and she visited
Mellifluous beyond my ardent reach, always off
Before me. I followed into rhythms I knew
Were good, her chamois softness weighing me
By morning toward a cozy common center.

She died there, when I was twelve.
I was sleeping, alien, down the hall

In a harder bed, isolated form the delicate
Destruction that took its year to take her.
That night my mother barely touched my hair
And in stiff, safe mechanics twirled the customary

Corners of my pillow one by one. "Grandma's gone,"
She said. Crepuscular against the only light
Alive behind her in the hall, she somehow left.
My covers fell like lonely lead on only me.
I lay as if in children's banks of white where
After new snow we plopped to stretch and carve

Our shapes like paper dolls along a fold.
Now, lying on my back, I ran my longest arms
From hip to head, slow arcs on icy sheets,
And whispered childhood's chant to the breathless room:
"Angel, Angel, snowy Angel,
Spread your wings and fly."

Gentle Then

Pity me not that she is gone
    to lean on tireless ages that solicit learning.
Pity me not that her frail self
    is quiet in my rooms.
Pity me not that I should wake
    to find inanimate what tangibles there are.

Instead, know tender joy with me
    that she enlivens every corner of my soul
    with having been
    and being still,
    coursing through my veins
    to tell me where I have to go,
    alive within me
    vibrant, real, and gentler even
    than she was gentle then.

And when I see her,
    as I surely will, herself again,
    we will be as loving close
    as on the aching day we said goodbye.

I Marry You

What was I?
What roused my day?
What pampered night?
What brought yellow roses hovering about
    like fairies that scampered
    from my childhood
    when the light went on
    but left their whimsy
    for my private eyes?
What is it that you bring?

What was I? What gave the salt,
    the burning clove?
    what rescued quietly abandoned dreams
    like plankton moving
    toward the unseen motion
    of a changing moon?
Where have you taken me?

Before the bringing
    and the taking,
what made me know enough
    to marry you?

To My Newborn Child

We lived together,
you and I,
fed from tables
where I chose with
unaccustomed caution
wanting vibrance
on a spoon
or strength by glass,
certain of your
tasting too.

Nights I willed
my possibles to you,
prayed whatever right
was in me
to be yours.
Mornings, meadow larks
and yellow sun
I filtered consciously
through layered pores
to let you
in your silent darkness
sense your daily
birthright.

Afternoons I ran us both
beyond the edges
sometimes pressed
by wisdom and propriety,
extending every boundary
that jealous time imposed.
Through private months
we grew
as one.

Now with sudden
brazen cry
you're shouting,
"I am one!"
And we are two,
you and I.
But one
as you must wait to know.

Child's Play

At one time I had sixteen dolls
accumulated over years of wanting them,
all comforted and put to be each night,
bathed each day and tendered,
while the tomboy in me tossed in deluded repose.

The dolls in their claim
eclipsed all but emerging. Something
in playing with them
made my motherhood authentic,
then and now, and taught me
long before the compounding of years
what holding meant.

So unambiguous that play,
so undemanding its demands,
so emblazoning the need to hold,
so right its rites,
that its celestial consummation in you, my child,
kindles like tremulous fire that childhood-tinted
awe
at being now Mother.

Sisters Giggling Somewhere

They laugh and laugh
at what I wish I understood.
Within them
is strung the ease of intimation,
the pure chaos of discovery,
the treasury of hours pressing back
the pummeling of ciphers and solemn figuring.

Theirs is the felicity of flowering.
They laugh without stint or exertion,
breathing in the day's distance,
breathing out the air pf peaches and mint.
Even their silence would be liquid
these 300 miles. But they sprinkle us
with the luminous dew of childhood.

Giggling becomes the scribble of laughter,
the nonsense that wriggles free,
prodigious in travel,
empty and flawless,
unfolding among us the limits
of fugitive grace.

Quick Freeze

It snowed last night, hooray! Hurrah!
The two-year-old beholds with awe,
And so she imposes her domination–
Till she's into the boots, the coat, the hat,
The mittens, the leggings, the this-and-that
Which launch her, a bundle of insulation.

And scarcely a mother is now alive
Who gets to count higher than maybe five
Till rosy and teary (this tale's so old!)
She begs to go in 'cause oh, it's cold!

The Good Hurt

She sits on her foot for a long long time
While she colors and cut with scissors.
And when she goes to walk again,
Her foot is filled with frizzers.
Each time she steps she feels the dots
The sparkle in her toes.
She thinks she needs a band-aid cure,
But there's not one thing that shows!

To Daughters Eight and Ten

Now girls, I'm aware you must wriggle and giggle
And for the hysterical search,
But please let your fun day be Monday not Sunday,
And don't start us laughing in church!

The Generation Gap

Remembering's simple, psychologist say–
Look back and remember feeling the way
Your child must feel. Then merely empathize,
Identify, isolate, concretize
Your subliminal sensitivity,
Which, exercised deftly, can be the key
To understanding, communication.
Externalize the whole situation.

Thus prodded, I plod through Spock and Gesell,
Determined, objective, and willing–Oh well!
Who am I kidding, no matter how dutiful–
How can I transfer? She's sixteen and beautiful!

Letter to a Daughter

My Dear:

You're living away from home for the first time. Meeting a galaxy of new and fascinating people, many of them talking up the freedom of their new morality and urging you to join them.

And you're listening–and wondering. And why not? After all, you are almost nineteen, attractive, interesting, sophisticated in some ways, gullible and easily led in other ways. More than anything right now, you want to explore, to see and feel and do everything that might enlarge your horizons, which suddenly can seem so cramped by home influences, tradition, and inexperience. Our town can look like a pretty small place.

So what do you say when confronted with differences, when plagued to defend your homespun no's? You don't have to defend your position, of course–you have every right just to say no. But I realize that you need something more than just a feeling to justify (for yourself anyhow) your rejection of so much that is made to look awfully appealing by the intellectual arguments of people whose ideas you usually respect. They say things like, "This is now." "Things have changed. The old moral codes have disintegrated in the new freedom." "Be open-minded. Don't be held down by old-fashioned, outmoded morals that no longer apply." "Don't knock a thing when you haven't tried it." "It's meaningful relationships that count now—not a bunch of biblical don'ts," and mostly, "Repression is abnormal–unhealthy."

And you're up-to-date—you respond to today with the eagerness and openness that are products of growing up in a decade of questioning and revolt, of rejection of the traditional. In all other areas, you are expected to entertain change as the most challenging and acceptable part of our maturing. Then why say no to a changing moral code that would dump you in bed with the next attractive interesting urgent male with whom you are "compatible"?

Maybe I can suggest some reasons for saying no that make sense to me–see how they work for you. A while ago you and I talked about a movie we had both seen (not together) in which casual sex was basic to the plot. With candor you said the story, while not representative of your way of life, was acceptable on the screen, yet to me it was unnerving–in fact, pretty degrading. Maybe our reactions to this movie were so different because we are at such different stages of our lives. For you, lovemaking is something yet to come, something talked about, maybe joked about, and certainly something anticipated as part of marriage. For me it is something very real, sanctified, and part of a good life. And that's what I want it to become for you.

But as I watch movies like that and read current novels and hear you and your sisters and friends talk, I want to say–wait a minute–just wait a minute! There's nothing better–and there can be nothing worse–than the expression of human sexuality, but for heaven's sake (and that works in two ways!) give yourself a chance to be totally human, totally alive, and totally satisfied with the experience. Isn't that what all the modern thinkers are advocating too? But my formula, and I know it works, is not one of capitulation to whim or circumstance. It takes some doing–some waiting but it pays off.

Maybe you could call it the "best of everything theory." Here's how it goes: Heavenly Father has made us his children. As such, we have tremendous capacities. We can enjoy life at many levels. There is little limit to our potential. And he has said that we are that we might have joy. So why shouldn't this be true with the life giving, fulfilling experience of making love?

The way I see it, a lot of people today are willing to settle for just the physical, and others for only the physical and emotional satisfactions, but it's jolly well a privilege to get all levels in one experience. It is possible, and it is what I want for you, of course.

If you just want the physical, then goodness knows it's easy to come by–sort of like hitting a pressure point with a hammer: anyone with a central nervous system intact will respond. Fine, it that's all you want–a quick reaction to a fleeting stimulus that could work with almost any two people anywhere. Pretty basic. Pretty frog-like.

If you want to move one step up, to enjoy an emotional involvement as well, then what you need to do is find someone who cares for you and for whom you care, at least for now. This can be achieved through very casual relationships and can produce an electric, if not lasting, encounter. At any rate, a combination of the physical and emotional is a step up from the purely physical in any scheme of things.

Suppose you're smart enough to want even more from this experience of making love, this experience which has forever furnished eloquence for the poet and fortunes for the filmmakers.

Suppose you want to slip a little mental stimulus and satisfaction into the brew. That means you need to have an alliance that your head would sanction as well as your heart. This requires someone you would choose in the cold calculations of daylight, someone who your brain says is right, not just someone who stirs you physically and emotionally. And sometimes this takes some searching. I once heard a marriage counselor say to a group: If you and your fiancé can spend a whole day together without once making any physical contact-and have a good time—you are probably in love, not just infatuated. And, dear, anytime you can elevate a relationship to move through the physical, the emotional, and the mental, you're off toward something good.

But being human and part of a society, you can expect even more from participating in the love act. You can enjoy a relationship that is honored and accepted and smiled on by those you care about. You can kiss in the sunlight, know genuine peace, and walk with your head high through your days after delighting in your nights. It's easy to flaunt society in the abstract, to say I don't care what people think. But we do. We all do. We care what people we care about think. But most important, there is tremendous strength in being committed to something of value, and society with its traditions and morals has furnished us an honorable, workable setting for much that is good, including lovemaking. There isn't a condition to compare with marriage for generating deep, meaningful, long-lasting, and devoted partnerships that make the partners and the world in which they exist better for their being.

Finally, as a child of God, you have every right to expect your lovemaking to comprise not only the best of these capacities–the impact of the physical, the thrill of the emotional, the assurance of the mental, and the comfort of the social–but you can expect as well the overriding bliss (and I say bliss advisedly, knowing how you feel about exaggeration) –yes, the bliss of spiritual confirmation of the most blessed and sacred of any human involvement. To have the approval of your Father in Heaven, to feel his pleasure, to know his blessing in that beautiful act, together with those wonderfully human and potent feelings—this is to know what love and lovemaking are really all about. Then too, to love without fear of becoming a family—in fact, to relish and anticipate that eventuality—is the most blessed of freedoms afforded two blessed human beings.

So I guess, dear middle child, that I'm just assuming, as you've taught me to assume, that you respect yourself and your potential enough to want it all—all that's possible to be had. You always have. You ski the hardest slopes, paint in the richest colors, and can never go to bed for wanting to taste more of the day. And you touch us all with the softness of loving us and life and the Giver of it all. How lucky I am to be
Your Mother
P.S. Be happy, my little girl grown up. I love you. And keep saying no till time to say yes–to the right marriage that you deserve and want. You'll be glad.

Goodnight

Softly aging here
I move from bed to bed
and measure out my tired time
in lengths along their languid,
covered legs.

Five daughters sleeping to my touch
spread across the pillows
honeyed to their hair –
and take my kiss in ways as
different
as their eyes and ages.

Eight balls up tighter,
nudges me, and sighs.
Fifteen startles wide and then
collapses into quiet recognition,
smiling. Seventeen hardly stirs
but breathes against my cheek some
gentle sound. Twelve tenses, turns,
and pulls me down in fierce acknowledgment.
And nineteen rolls away to cover up my
brazen tattoo
on her cheek.

I move toward the stairs
vulnerable, divided into fifths,
and come to you
to be made whole.

Cure

Hurt, too old to cry the salt out of the wound,
you walk away from me, snapping at the rescues
offered out of love that used to rescue.

Bewildering in frantic fantasies, you besiege
your private corners, retreats with doorless walls
where no one (not even they) can pummel you
with positives.

I watch you go with mother's certainties spilling
into the quick sands of your time. I strip aching
sudden years away and rush to grownup gashes
with foolish band-aids in my hand.

Hold

Only one more Sunday and she'll be gone.
But now she plays her violin, old songs
That drew her from the squawking bow to
trembling
Sweetness that singes these last frayed, jumbled
Days with aching suspension. Not return.
No, not even to the solid blurting
Years of simple acquiescence to demand—
The changing, feeding, cleaning, running strands
That lay upon each other, patterning
This closeness into womanhood, flattening
Our prints into this time of hard goodbye.
Unbreathed, just holding. To suffocate the sigh
That will wisp her off to some strange place for
Drawing music from new strings and score.

Mother's Day

Hey, World! Good morning.
Today I'm up for sure.
Watch me swing out of bed
and put my hand to everything
not where it should be! Dirty clothes,
you're sunk. Weeds, hang onto your roots.
Hunger, you'll be fed—by me, myself.
Personally I'll stir juice and beat with a wooden
spoon
and indulge any fancy that
makes it past the stairs.

Take me off. Spirit me away
through petunias and geraniums
and the birch that never really learned
how to cry. I'll catch whatever
you can throw and pin it high
on the grey grapestake that
fences not a thing.

Somewhere My Children

I never get used to the absence.
I close my eyes
but some clock pecks at the dark
and a lost firefly threads his strangeness
over my covered leg.
Where are you, my children,
nebulous as night,
stirring in my crevices?
Without ages you come for me.
You reach and run
and smile on my entreaties
never staying anyone the same.
You sift the years like
cinnamon in sugar
swirling through yourselves
and tumbling onto me
until I cannot breathe
for wanting to be home.

Lesson #1

(Featured in the 2002 Olympic Games)

Ski here,
my child,
not on gentle
slopes where
the snow is
packed and
the trail
is wide.
Instead
cut through
the trees where
no one's tried the
powder. Push toward
the hill and rotate as
you rise. No, the
snowplow holds
you back;
it's slow
and makes
you frightened
of your turn.
Think parallel.
Stay all in one,

then learn to ski
   the fall line, always
    down: Switchback
       skiers in their
         caution
           never know
             how dropping
              with the mountain
               keeps the balance
               right and rhythm
               smooth. Don't
              watch your
           tips
          at all!
        Look past
       them at the
     deep white snow,
     virgin as light,
       and yours.
        Just bend,
          release:
             You,
              gravity,
               and white will
                 make your peace.

Son-in-law

I wondered how it would be
to have a boy. Not a single one
but many: A soft one
to swaddle in kisses
without reservation.
One of fine threads concealed
in the spareness of cowboys.
One with daring arms able
to edify the exultation
of movement.
One with a welter of impulses,
extravagant and virile
in gentle comings and goings.
One with forbearance
of the tottering world
and the tentative gestures
hoping for love.
One with audacity
but no show of bravado,
no mask of pedigree,
no weaponry except instinct, himself
and faith for survival.
One animated by the simplest of things:
school bells, the silk of a petal,
the touch of a string, the lash of an ideal.

One to make beautiful passes
at the blazing secrets
and come up cherishing the earth.
There was no reason to improvise
what I never had.
Only to wait
in my sea of days
and the bounty of my daughters.
Some other island
fashioned this singular son,
all of it in him,
to liven like a barrage of salt
these years
trembling with passing.

Prospect: My Child with Child

I remember the terrible joy,
    the groping of the unplumbed
    for signs,
        as if some new nerves would sear somewhere
        in annunciation.
The awakening at any hour
    first to "Who is there?"
        then "Where?"
        and "Do you know, you too?"
Some shimmer licked my inner sides
    with long exploratory tongues of testing
    whether I could hold my own.
Now having held
    and held,
    I hear you who occupied that place
    tell of your shimmerings,
    and a fire crazes me
    with vacant fullness
        on this night when I remember
        with the brightness of your dark eyes.

Here I Love You

Here I love you
in the waves of the fire
lifting its first heat
through last night's blue morning.

I love you among these cold things
when I get up early
to fold my dreams into the chimney
and all but my soul
is still sleeping.

I love you in tawny lithe remembering,
the sun yellow in a bright pool
of your breathing.
you are here
in the unfinished things
that are done,
in the rough roof that raises long tongues
to sing to me.

Here I love you
in my life before and after anyone.
if my voice does not reach you
let me send you my silence
to tell you
where I am.

Bathing a First Grandchild, Three Months Old, at the Cabin

Grandson Nicholas Thayne Markosian
I will bathe you in fastidious bubbles,
carve the nails of your flying hands into the
    circles of your mother's becoming.
I will carry the canyon tub wrinkled with dents
to the porch where the sun will fill it
with nonsense, and you and I
will rollick in water warmed
from my far-off drinkable stream.
I will bless your father
in the spanable silk of your back
and call to every ancestor
To relish your toes. Little Buddha,
you'll splash your turkey pink whimsy
into the froth of my kisses
and clutch at what's left of me
dangling before you my happiest face.

In the long towel you'll be Moses
blinking in front of your smile.
I will spread the splendor of loving

over your soft surfaces
and press your addictive rounds into my
    chaste restorations.
Then I will dress you slowly
In the fragrance of unspoken words
And curl you into the cave
Of my confident arm
To sleep.

Gift

"Mom and I, we're pretty much the same,"
she said once in a poem when she was ten.
And oh, the burden of the joy to know
what more she was than sameness even then:

"Sunfilled" is what she called herself,
  Sun filled.

About the Author

Emma Lou Warner Thayne grew up with her three brothers on horses, lakes, ski slopes, and tennis courts. A former college poetry instructor and coach of the University of Utah Women's Tennis Team, she was ranked #3 nationally in the 50-and-over doubles. Her articles, short stories and poems have won numerous distinctions and have been widely anthologized. A few of her many honors include: David O. MacKay humanities award from Brigham Young University; Honorary Doctorate and Distinguished Alumna, University of Utah; The Thayne Center for Service and Learning at Salt Lake Community College bears her name; writing and poetry awards from The Association for Mormon Letters; The Governors Commission for Women and Families: Utah Woman of Achievement Award in Recognition of a Lifetime of Contribution and Service; Cathedral of Madeleine Award for distinguished Service to the Arts and humanities.